A Nostalgic Piece
for flute and piano

ELENA KATS-CHERNIN

20210601

2

Elena Kats-Chernin

A Nostalgic Piece
for flute and piano

2013

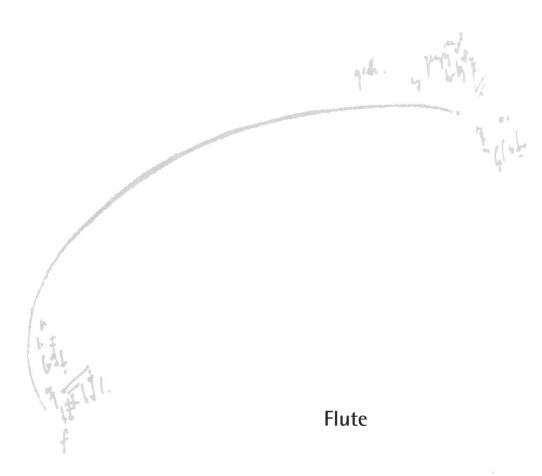

Flute

BOOSEY & HAWKES
BOTE & BOCK

Flute

A Nostalgic Piece
for flute and piano

ELENA KATS-CHERNIN

20210601

arranged from the violin and piano version
by Christine Draeger, September 2013

ISMN 979-0-2025-3486-1

9 790202 534861

ISBN 978-3-7931-4183-9

9 783793 141839

BOOSEY & HAWKES
BOTE & BOCK

*arranged from the violin and piano version
by Christine Draeger, September 2013*

20210601

Elena Kats-Chernin
A Nostalgic Piece
for flute and piano
(2013)

Duration: 3′

www.boosey.com

BB 3486

ISMN 979-0-2025-3486-1
ISBN 978-3-7931-4183-9